Made in the USA
Coppell, TX
21 July 2021

59261925R00066